BUYING A SECONDHAND YACHT

EDMUND WHELAN
Barrister-at-Law

Published by the Royal Yachting Association

CONTENTS

INTRODUCTION

The purchase of a yacht is probably the second biggest investment the average owner will make in his life. Even a relatively modest cruiser capable of going offshore is likely to cost tens of thousands of pounds, while a yacht large enough to cross an ocean in real comfort, with a few home luxuries aboard, will cost well over a hundred thousand.

And yet for all the expense and risk involved, the legal side of buying a yacht can be as simple as buying a box of matches.

The Merchant Shipping Act defines a "ship" as "any description of vessel not propelled by oars". Thus any yacht is a ship, even down to the smallest sailing dinghy or powerboat. By the same token, any yacht owned by a British National is a British ship, entitled to registration on one of the British shipping registers, and also to all the rights and liabilities attaching to registered British ships under the Merchant Shipping Acts.

Unlike buying a house, it is possible for a yacht to pass through many hands, from one owner to another, without ever being registered, or without registration details being changed on each change of ownership. This is because a yacht is a chattel, rather than real property (like a house) and because registration is voluntary (unlike a motor vehicle where the Road Traffic Acts require every change of ownership to be notified to the Vehicle Licensing Authority).

The absence of formality does not in any way imply that the buyer of a yacht does not obtain good title. Although the first owner buying a new yacht will probably receive a Builder's Certificate and a receipted invoice from the builder or dealer, in many cases these documents are mislaid and subsequent buyers will often (unwisely) take over the yacht by a simple verbal agreement and no documentation.

Although a yacht can be bought and sold without formality and used without being registered, this is definitely not recommended. The purchase and use of a yacht is full of potentially expensive pitfalls for the uninitiated and experienced alike; the purpose of this book is to identify those pitfalls and guide the buyer on how to protect his investment and his peace of mind.

1

THE CONTRACT

It is a common fallacy among non-lawyers that a contract needs to be in writing to be binding on either party to an agreement. In fact this is not the case except for the sale of "real property" (i.e. land, or a house) where the Law of Property Act specifically requires contracts to be in writing. A simple conversation on the following lines:

A. "I like the look of your yacht, how much would you sell her for?

B. She's yours for twenty thousand pounds

A. All right, I'll buy her for twenty thousand pounds,"

is sufficient to create a binding contract or agreement (the words are interchangeable).

So far as the seller is concerned, the simpler the deal the better. His only interest is to receive the money as soon as possible and shed his responsibilities for the care and upkeep of the yacht.

For the buyer however, the results of a quick verbal agreement of that sort could be absolutely disastrous. Unless he can be sure that the yacht and all the fittings are in good condition, that all VAT and taxes due on the yacht have been paid, that there are no yard, marina or salvage bills outstanding, that all the equipment to be sold with the yacht has been listed and agreed, that there are no outstanding mortgages or legal charges on the yacht, that all co-owners agree to the sale, and that the actual ownership of the yacht will not pass to him before he has arranged full insurance cover, he could be making a very expensive mistake.

However, a methodical approach to buying the yacht, leaving out any potentially expensive shortcuts, should ensure that most of these risks are minimised; the size of the investment obviously justifies a thoroughly cautious and even suspicious approach, unless both yacht and seller are well known to the buyer.

The starting point for the buyer will be one of the standard form contracts available either from the broker (if one is involved in selling the yacht), or from the Royal Yachting Association (reproduced in Appendix 1).

Bearing in mind the risk of entering into a binding agreement by a verbal offer and acceptance, the careful buyer will ensure that no commitment is made on his part until he has satisfied himself on every aspect of the purchase.

Having found the yacht of his choice, and before negotiating the price, he should make it clear to the seller that, if an offer is made, it will be subject to a written contract being entered into. Where the buyer intends to enter into a face to face bargaining session, it would be advisable to have two copies of the standard form contract ready to hand, so that the session can finish with both parties signing the contract and being bound by its terms.

Once the price has been settled, the precise terms of the inventory agreed, and all other points fully understood by both parties, the relevant parts of the written contract should be completed, and the documents signed, with each party taking a copy for his own use.

The standard form contract is reprinted in full at Appendix 1; it is important that both parties understand fully the matters that are dealt with in the contract, and the way in which the transaction proceeds under the terms of the contract. The contractual terms are laid out in the following sequence.

PARTIES

It may seem an obvious point, but both the vendor and the purchaser need to be sure exactly who is buying and who is selling the yacht. It is important that any joint owner of the vendor is disclosed, and if the yacht is to be bought in the name of another person (or company) this should be written into the contract.

PURCHASE PRICE AND DEPOSIT

The conventional deposit is 10% of the agreed purchase price but there is no reason why the purchaser should not offer a lesser sum and amend the contract accordingly. The purchase price, once agreed, is of course binding on both parties unless the purchaser is able to rely on Clause 5 of the contract (defects disclosed by survey) to offer a lower sum. In that case it is for the vendor to decide whether to accept or reject the lower offer.

AGREEMENT FOR SALE

The vendor's agreement to sell carries the legal implication that he has the right to sell, and that the yacht is free of any encumbrances, charges, liens etc. This is referred to in more detail in Clause 7.3 and is also enforceable under Section 12 of the Sale of Goods Act 1979. Advice on checking the vendor's title is given in Chapter 4.

THE YACHT AND EQUIPMENT

It may be that the vendor wishes to retain the name for his next yacht. If the yacht is on the Part 1 Register (see Chapter 3) the requirement for a unique name means that the purchaser will have to contract to change the name of the yacht after completion.

It is important for the purchaser to make an inventory of the machinery, equipment and gear as early as possible in the proceedings, as loose items worth many hundreds, even thousands of pounds, have a habit of walking once a price has been agreed. The inventory forms part of the contract and should be initialled by both parties after a joint inspection.

VALUE ADDED TAX AND OTHER DUES

Many thousands of yachts are lying in overseas marinas and harbours, being used regularly by their owners, but without local VAT or other dues having been paid. Some overseas authorities are content with the situation until the yacht is sold, when the claim for VAT and dues might be backed up with the impounding of the yacht. Further advice is given in Chapter 5.

INSPECTION/SURVEY

A survey is considered essential by most owners, and the contract is designed to provide a period between signing of the contract and completion for the survey to take place. Typically the purchaser will ask for 21 days to arrange a survey, but where both parties are keen to complete the transaction quickly, a surveyor can be instructed at a few days notice and requested to prepare a written report immediately after the survey. This need only take 2 or 3 days, depending on the availability of an experienced and qualified professional. Further advice on surveys is given in Chapter 2. It should be noted that all expenses involved in a survey, including yard fees and preparing the yacht for survey, are met by the purchaser.

NOTICE OF DEFECTS/ACCEPTANCE OF YACHT

The survey will normally disclose material defects that had not previously been seen on the purchaser's inspection. This will give the purchaser the opportunity to reject the yacht, cancel the contract and claim his deposit back, or propose to the vendor a lower price or the opportunity for the vendor to remedy the defects. The vendor of course has the right to reject a lower offer or a notice to remedy the defects and to look for an alternative purchaser. The contract provides a strict time framework for both the purchaser and the vendor to take action after the survey, and both should bear these time limits in mind at all times.

COMPLETION OF SALE

The purchaser is required to pay the balance of the agreed price within seven days of the acceptance of the yacht.

If the yacht is on the Part 1 Register (see Chapter 3) the vendor should hand over the ship's papers at this time. In addition to the Certificate of Registry and Bill of Sale these should include the Builder's Certificate, the original VAT invoice, all contracts and Bills of Sale tracing ownership of the yacht from new to the present transaction, and all equipment manuals and service records. In practice many vendors are unable to produce much in the way of paperwork, but a valid Certificate of Registry, Bill of Sale, and proof of VAT payment or exemption (see Chapter 5) should be regarded as essential.

If the yacht is unregistered or on the Small Ships Register (see Chapter 3) proof of VAT payment or exemption, and a simple Bill of Sale is all that is required. This may be as reproduced at Appendix 5.

VENDOR'S RIGHT TO ASSIGN TITLE

See under *Agreement for Sale* above. However, even though the vendor guarantees under this section that he has the right to sell, and that the yacht is free from any charge, the checks outlined in Chapter 4 should still be carried out.

FREE ACCESS AFTER COMPLETION

A yacht laid up ashore may have easy access at the time of the purchaser's initial inspection, but by the time completion has taken place the yacht may be blocked in by numerous other craft being laid up. Removal of the yacht by the purchaser's contractors can mean great additional expense as yachts are shuffled around the yard to make space for the removal.

WARRANTIES

This section underlines the importance of a survey in buying a yacht from a private individual. **The Sale of Goods Act provisions about merchantable quality and fitness for purpose do not apply to private sales** and the vendor is under no duty to draw defects to the attention of the purchaser. If the vendor has made specific representations, statements, or promises about the yacht, that is a different matter, but proving such statements in court on a misrepresentation case is likely to be very much more costly and time consuming than commissioning a professional survey.

RISK
It is important that the risk in the yacht should not pass to the purchaser until he has completed his insurance arrangements (see Chapter 7).

DEFAULT
The contract provides for the rights of each party in the event of a default by the other. One point which over-optimistic purchasers often fail to realise until it is too late is that there is no provision in the contract for changes of mind. Once the contract is signed, and unless the survey discloses previously unseen material defects, the purchaser is bound to proceed with the transaction or risk losing his deposit and any additional costs (including the shortfall in price offered by a later purchaser) involved in a re-sale.

ARBITRATION
If a dispute does arise, it is preferable for the parties to agree to an informal arbitration before instructing solicitors. Legal proceedings should only be entered into after all other avenues of conciliation have been explored.

ENTIRE AGREEMENT CLAUSE
The final clause in the contract provides that no other written or verbal statements should be taken into account by either party in interpreting the contract. This does not prevent the purchaser from taking legal action in respect of any misrepresentation by the vendor by which he was persuaded to enter into the contract. A representation does not form part of the contract and is not affected by this clause.

2

THE SURVEY

Provision is made in Clause 4 of the contract for the purchaser to have the yacht surveyed. Although the yacht may appear to be in excellent condition,. and a survey may appear unnecessary, it is a sensible precaution to take. A surveyor will usually find sufficient hidden problems with the yacht to enable the buyer to reduce his first offer by at least the equivalent of the surveyor's fees; in more serious cases he can detect signs of potentially disastrous defects, and in any event his report will provide some level of guarantee since he will be legally liable for the costs of remedying any defects that he has negligently missed.

The detailed instructions given to the surveyor are of importance. It may simply be that a hull condition survey is required, or a full survey to include rig, sails, engine and all other equipment aboard. If the engine or engines form a substantial part of the value of the boat, it will probably be worthwhile having a separate detailed engineers report, which may include a sea trial and full report on the yacht's performance.

The surveyor should also be given a copy of the particulars of sale and asked to verify any technical aspects, or references to measurements, that are important to the buyer.

Once the survey and engineers report (if any) have been received, the contract allows the buyer up to 14 days to decide on his next step. If the survey discloses no material defects, then the buyer is obliged to go ahead with the agreement. If on the other hand material defects are found which were not readily apparent on the buyer's initial inspection of the yacht, he has the option either of withdrawing from the sale and having his deposit refunded, renegotiating the price to allow for repairs or renewals, or requesting the seller to rectify matters at his own expense prior to completion of the contract.

Whether a defect is material or not is a frequent source of dispute between the parties. Although there is no exact definition as to what is material, it could be said that if the cost of remedying the defect or defects is more than 5% of the agreed value of the yacht then that is definitely material, below that percentage it becomes more arguable according to the specific defect concerned.

When selecting a surveyor or engineer it is advisable to

establish whether they have full professional indemnity insurance. The likelihood of a surveyor failing to detect a serious fault may be limited, but mistakes can be made and unless the surveyor carries insurance the buyer may find himself without financial redress. Most surveyors are members of a professional body such as the Royal Institute of Naval Architects or the Institute of Marine Engineers. There are however many who hold no formal qualifications but whose experience more than makes up for this. Membership of the Yacht Brokers, Designers and Surveyors Association is limited to those with relevant qualifications or experience, and indeed the YBDSA insists on all its surveying members carrying full professional indemnity insurance.

In bygone days the majority of yachts were built under Lloyds supervision, and this body still enjoys a worldwide reputation. However, in recent years a number of cases have arisen where the buyer of a yacht with a Lloyds certificate has found to his cost that it does not provide a full guarantee and financial indemnity against defects. There is no substitute for the buyer instructing his own surveyor and having a report prepared for his own purposes. A report prepared for another person may appear to cover all the buyer's points of concern, but it is unlikely that the buyer could take legal action against a negligent surveyor unless the report was prepared for him, on his own instructions.

3

REGISTRATION

As we have seen, registration for any size of pleasure craft within the United Kingdom is entirely voluntary. An owner may wish to register his craft for a number of different reasons, his reasons will dictate the form of registration he chooses.

PART 1 REGISTRATION

The Merchant Shipping Act 1894, Part 1 lays down full procedures for the registration of any British ship. Registration under Part 1 which is managed at 14 regional centres by HM Customs and Excise requires full details and proof of ownership to be provided by the applicant, together with a measurement survey report prepared by a qualified tonnage measurer. With measurement fee, certification fee, and the required marking of the vessel with the registered number, the total cost of registration is, at 1993 prices, over £400. However, since registration under Part 1 provides the owner with unquestionable proof of title, it can make the later sale of the yacht very much simpler, as a purchaser need only satisfy himself that the seller is the registered owner, and the yacht is not subject to a registered mortgage.

SMALL SHIPS REGISTER

The SSR was instituted in 1983 in response to the requirement of a number of overseas authorities for British owned yachts to be properly registered, and the reluctance of many yacht owners to pay the full registration fee required. The SSR provides a yacht owner going foreign with a Government issued document stating the name of the declared owner. The certificate is issued simply upon the completion of a form by the applicant and is of no value as proof, or even evidence, of ownership. However, since the cost is £10 for a 5 year certificate and entitles the registered owner to wear a privileged ensign (provided he is a member of a relevant club) and to carry duty free stores (if taking his yacht beyond the "Home Trade Limits" of Brest to Elbe), there are a great number of yacht owners who opt for Small Ships Registration in preference to Part 1 Registration.

CHECKING THE REGISTER

For the prospective purchaser, checking the registers is the first and most obvious step that should be taken.

For a yacht on the Part 1 Register, the name and Port of Registry (or initials of the owner's club) should be marked on the stern, and the official number either carved in the main beam (at the deckhead adjacent to the main mast) of a wooden yacht, or displayed on a plaque on the main bulkhead in the case of a grp or metal-hulled yacht. The owner should also be able to show a certificate naming him as the registered owner. Having satisfied himself that the yacht is the one referred to (including a check on the engine serial number) the buyer should then contact the Registrar at the Port of Registry and request a transcript of the registration particulars. This transcript should duplicate the information on the registration certificate, and in addition will also disclose whether any mortgage has been placed on the vessel. The buyer should beware however, since the Register does not allow for the reservation of title and, in theory, it is possible for an unscrupulous seller to enter into a mortgage agreement with a finance house (or even sell the yacht to another buyer) between the buyer's inspection of the register and completion of the sale, particularly if there is a delay between the two. It is for this reason that the buyers of large ships normally require the transaction to take place in the Registrar's office with the Register open on the table for all parties to see as the money (in banker's draft form) changes hands. The address and telephone number if the principal Register of Shipping in London is given at Appendix 6.

For yachts on the Small Ships Register there is very little real purpose in checking the registration particulars, since the information on that Register is simply an unverified duplicate of the information originally supplied by the applicant.

TRANSFER OF TITLE

Once the buyer has completed his investigations of title and acted upon the results of the survey he will usually wish to go ahead with completion of the sale. Whether this is through a broker or privately he should not hand over the final balance of the purchase price unless he is given the relevant documentation to enable him to re-register the yacht in his own name. In the case of a Part 1 registered yacht, this will consist of the yacht's registration certificate in the seller's name, and a Bill of Sale made out in the name of the buyer and signed by the registered owner. If either of these is defective it will not be possible for the buyer to re-register the yacht in his own name, and he will often be put to great trouble and expense in remedying the problem. If the seller is unable at the last minute to produce exactly the right documentation, then the buyer should consider retaining a part of the price (perhaps 5% or 10% of the total) against receipt of the required documentation.

It often happens for example that a seller did not take the trouble to re-register the yacht in his own name when he originally acquired it. This does not signify that his beneficial ownership of the yacht is in doubt, but it would involve the new buyer having to trace the original registered owner to persuade him to sign the Bill of Sale in his favour. If this proves impossible (as is often the case) the buyer will have no option but to make a formal application to the High Court for an order requiring the Registrar to transfer the title. These problems can be reduced by simple precautions at the time of completion.

Once the buyer has the Certificate of Registry and a Bill of Sale in his possession, these should be sent to the Registrar with the appropriate fee for change of particulars (£80 in 1993). An amended certificate will be sent back to the new owner in due course.

For yachts on the Small Ships Register the procedure is very much simpler. Since the Register entry and certificate are not evidence of title, the only check that can be carried out is an inspection of the Certificate for any sight of obvious fraud and an enquiry to the SSR Office.

The cautious buyer will also carry out further checks as referred to in Chapter 4.

On completion of the sale the buyer does not need to obtain any specific documentation, although either the signed contract, a copy of the original VAT receipt or exemption certificate, a receipt for the money, or a completed Bill of Sale will help if kept with the ship's papers and produced as evidence of title when he comes to sell the yacht on in due course.

4

CHECKING THE VENDOR'S TITLE

As we have seen, there is no legal requirement for a yacht owner to record his ownership on either of the official registers. This obviously has implications for a buyer when purchasing a yacht from a stranger, since in many cases he will not be sure that the seller has a *bona fide* right to sell, or that the yacht does not have a loan outstanding against it, which could (and all too often does) lead to it being repossessed by the finance company from the new owner.

PART 1 REGISTERED YACHTS

For yachts that are entered on the Part 1 Register, the position is relatively simple. A buyer can satisfy himself that the yacht is indeed the property of the alleged owner, and that there are no registered mortgages entered on the register, simply by contacting the Registrar at the Port of Registry and asking for a transcript of the Register entry for that yacht. This is obtainable by post at a cost of £25 and the transcript will show who the registered owner is, and for how long he has been the registered owner, as well as any registered mortgages (name of lender only, not the amount of the original mortgage nor the amount outstanding).

LIENS

The buyer should however remember that although the entry on the Register indicates good title, and any unregistered mortgages are invalid against a *bona fide* purchaser without notice of them, it is still possible for other parties to have a lien or interest in the yacht. Harbour Authorities, marinas, boat repair yards, crew, salvors (if the yacht has been the subject of a salvage claim) victuallers, suppliers of equipment, or others, may all have a claim against the owner of a yacht, in which case they may also be able to claim a lien against the yacht itself, even when it has changed hands. This also extends to the VAT collection authorities if the yacht is VAT unpaid (or if the owner cannot prove that there is no VAT liability). It is of course impossible for an intending buyer to be completely satisfied that there are no liens outstanding on the yacht; the best he can do is ensure that the contract is signed (Clause 7.3 deals with liens, mortgages etc) and ask at the marina office, or the Harbour Master's Office if there are any known problems with the yacht. Word of any unpaid bills, marina charges, harbour dues or salvage claims tends to circulate very fast, and the local grapevine is probably the best means of accessing this information.

YACHTS ON THE SMALL SHIPS REGISTER

The SSR was set up by the Department of Transport under the Merchant Shipping Act 1983 for the simple purpose of providing an inexpensive alternative to Part 1 Registration for yachts going foreign. As we have seen (Chapter 3) registration of a yacht on the SSR is a simple matter of the owner filling in an application form and forwarding it to the DVLA. The Register is not intended to be a title register, or even to be evidence of ownership, and a registration certificate carries a warning to this effect.

For yachts registered on the SSR, or yachts that are unregistered, there is no simple means by which a prospective purchaser can check the seller's title, or check that there is no financial charge on the yacht. Therefore, unless the seller and the yacht are known to the buyer, it makes sense to investigate the title, even if the sale is through a reputable broker, since he is under no duty to run any checks on the seller's *bona fides*.

Ideally the seller should be able to produce documents of title showing the chain of ownership from the time the yacht was built, down to the present time. These should include the original Builder's Certificate, the original receipted VAT invoice from the builder, and subsequent signed forms of contract and Bills of Sale from the first owner to the second, and so on until the present owner. The seller may also be able to produce a file of recent receipts in his name for mooring charges, harbour dues, insurance premiums, and maintenance and repair work; if these are consistent with what is known about the seller and the yacht, and go back three or more years, then it is reasonable to assume that the yacht is his to sell. Even if the seller is entirely lacking in any documentary evidence of his ownership, (and this is not unusual), he should still be able to refer the buyer to a yacht club officer, a Harbour Master, a river or canal authority, or a boatyard. Except in the case of the very smallest boats moved from place to place on a trailer, any seller who is unable to refer a buyer to someone reliable in authority or in the boating business should be treated with caution.

Checking on the absence of an unregistered mortgage is a rather more difficult matter. In the recent High Court case of *The Shizelle* (1992), it was held that an unregistered mortgage on an unregistered yacht was valid not only against the original borrower, but also against any subsequent owner whether or not he knew of the mortgage. Given that a number of leading finance houses lend considerable sums of money on the basis of unregistered mortgages, this creates an obvious danger for buyers. In recent years an increasing number of cases have occurred where a buyer in good faith has had his boat repossessed by the defaulting seller's finance house. In some cases this does not occur until months or years after the sale, and is typically precipitated by the seller missing one or more of his repayment instalments.

In 1991/92 the RYA promoted the idea of a central record of unregistered mortgages with the leading lenders with the purpose of providing a single reference point for intending buyers to find out whether any of the participating finance houses had an interest in a particular boat.

However the scheme was shelved in 1992 to await a more favourable economic climate.

Thus the intending purchaser who wishes to take a thorough approach still needs to approach a number of different lenders to enquire if they have a charge on a particular yacht. Although there are in theory an enormous number of potential lenders, in practice an approach to each of the 5 lenders listed in Appendix 4, who between them probably cover 95% of the small yacht unregistered mortgage finance market, is as much as the prudent buyer can reasonably do to cover himself against this risk.

5

VAT LIABILITIES

Value Added Tax was introduced in the United Kingdom in 1972, as a tax on the supply of services, and on the sale or import of goods. Any yachts built in or imported into this country for private use since that date should be VAT-paid and ideally a seller of a yacht should be in a position to provide the buyer with the yacht's original VAT receipt, or at least a copy certified by the builder or original supplier as being a true copy. Unless the seller is able to produce proof that VAT on the yacht has been paid at some time, either in the United Kingdom or elsewhere in the EC, the buyer should be ready to face a potential VAT assessment on the current value of the yacht at any time an EC Customs official carries out a spot check.

Until the end of 1992 it was possible for a yacht built in the UK, for a UK resident, to be exported immediately upon completion without payment of VAT, for use overseas on a tax-free basis. The International Convention on Temporary Importation provided that all convention countries should permit the free use of recreational equipment and "means of transport" for touristic purposes for a minimum of six months in any one year. This rule was interpreted more liberally than the minimum in most European countries including France, Spain and Italy, and over the years tens of thousands of yachts built for northern European owners enjoyed tax free status in Mediterranean marinas.

The completion of the Single Financial Market on 1st January 1993 saw the end of concessions of this sort between EC States. Apart from a few months' grace for yachts already enjoying tax-free status, any yacht in any EC State, owned by a national of any EC State for his private use, must be VAT-paid. In theory it should make little difference which State the VAT is paid in, since rates are intended to be roughly equivalent (see Appendix 7 for details of 1993 rates). In practice however, experience has shown that some States tend to be considerably more flexible in agreeing modest valuations with owners, and allowing payments to be spread over an extended period. At the time of writing, the Customs and Excise authorities in the UK are apparently not prepared to discuss valuations or payment terms unless a yacht is actually within the UK (by which time it is obviously too late to negotiate). The importer of a yacht from outside the EC will therefore find it to his advantage to import it first to another EC State where a valuation and payment terms have been agreed in advance (in writing) before bringing it into this country. Once a yacht has been imported into any EC State and VAT paid, in theory no further VAT liability can arise within the EC.

The completion of the Single Financial Market on 1st January 1993 also saw the introduction of an amnesty for any yacht in the EC area built on or before 31st December 1984. Therefore unless a yacht owner in the EC is able to prove

> **either** that the yacht is VAT paid
> **or** that it was built before 31st December 1984
> **and** was in EC waters on 31/12/92 - 1/1/93,

he is liable to pay VAT on the current value of the yacht, and there are likely to be spot checks in any EC State on any yacht at any time.

The potential VAT liability is something that all intending purchasers must be aware of. If the seller of the yacht cannot produce full documentary evidence of non-VAT liability, then arguably the yacht is worth only 100/117 of the asking price.

A simplified form of proof of non-VAT liability is now available in all EC States. Known as the "Single Administrative Document" this is issued in the UK by HM Customs and Excise on request to any owner of a UK based yacht who is able to produce sufficient documentary evidence. The inclusion of the document in the ships papers will considerably simplify things when the yacht is subjected to the inevitable spot checks in the UK and other EC States in the future. Details of the SAD and advice on the documentary evidence required can be obtained from HM Customs and Excise and the RYA Legal Department (members only).

6

RAISING THE MONEY

Most buyers will have to make arrangements to borrow the necessary funds from a bank, building society, finance house or some other source.

If the borrowing requirement is relatively modest (relative, that is, to the income of the purchaser) and it is expected to clear the debt quickly, a simple bank overdraft will usually be the most convenient option. If it is likely to take the buyer more than 12 months to pay the loan off, for amounts up to about £5000, a bank will usually try to sell a personal loan plan; for larger sums a variable loan rate, pegged to the bank's base rate, will be offered.

High street banks do not normally take mortgages over privately owned yachts, partly because the technicalities of registering a marine mortgage are outside their normal experience, and partly because the high cost of formal registration on the Register of Shipping and formal notification of the mortgage. For sums in excess of about £15,000 however, they may well look for a first or second charge over the borrower's house. A rate of 3½ to 4% above the base rate may be asked for a secured loan, although this is always open to negotiation particularly in periods of financial uncertainty when borrowers are in shorter supply than funds.

In recent years building societies have become very much more competitive in the personal loan market, and experience has shown that they tend to be more flexible and understanding when a borrower's cash flow makes it difficult to keep up the repayment schedule. This is not to say that funds should ever be borrowed without a clear idea of how the money is to be repaid, but financial uncertainties can disrupt the best laid plans and a supportive borrower can often make the difference between survival and bankruptcy.

However the main players in the market are the specialist finance houses of which Lombard North Central, Mercantile Credit and NWS Bank are still the leaders, but with a number of other specialists who are often able to provide attractive deals.

The advantage of dealing with a specialist house is the availability of specific plans for marine finance and staff who are solely engaged in that area of business. When dealing with loans of £10,000 or more, the finance houses will generally take a mortgage over the yacht. The additional security provided by the mortgage will enable them to offer an interest rate comparing favourably with a bank's unsecured loan rate.

MARINE MORTGAGE

Money has been raised on the security of ships for as long as there have been shipping and banking industries. The traditional method of mortgaging a ship (and the legal definition of ship includes "any vessel not propelled by oars") is by way of a formal charge on the Register of British Ships established under Part 1 of the 1894 Merchant Shipping Act. One of the main reasons for registering a yacht under the Part 1 Register, rather than the simpler and cheaper Small Ships Register, is to provide the basis for a formal mortgage to be arranged. No mortgage recording facility exists on the Small Ships Register.

The effect of a mortgage in favour of a financial institution is not to transfer ownership to the lender, but simply to restrict the borrower to using the yacht in a way that will not prejudice the lender's security. Thus the mortgage agreement will usually include clauses about chartering, lending, parting with possession, part sales of shares in the yacht, and of course insurance. In the case of a default in mortgage repayments the agreement will invariably allow the lender to repossess the yacht without any of the formalities, or protective provisions, that the owner of a private house may be entitled to.

Even after default and repossession however, the law allows the borrower an equitable right to redeem the security by paying off what is owing. In such a case the court will make an order directing that the accounts between parties should be finalised and that if the mortgagor fails to pay the sum due within a certain period (normally six months) then the mortgage will be foreclosed and the mortgagee (lender) will become the absolute owner of the property.

UNREGISTERED MORTGAGES

As we have seen, yachts registered on the Small Ships Register are not capable of being mortgaged under the procedures in the Merchant Shipping Acts. Although most financial institutions, particularly in the case of large mortgages on high value yachts, will insist on full Part 1 Registration and recording of a statutory mortgage, a number will now offer an unregistered mortgage facility to borrowers with very much less formality involved.

This form of unregistered mortgage is intended to provide the lender with a comparable degree of security to that provided under the Part 1 Register. Apart from the obvious cost advantage; (the requirement for Part 1 Registration would cost the borrower at least £350 in addition to the £80 mortgage registration fee, compared with a £10 registration fee for the Small Ships Register), an unregistered mortgage works in such a way as to vest actual title in the yacht to the lender. Arguably this is a better form of security for the lender than the simple charge allowed by a statutory mortgage, and lending rates for unregistered mortgages are generally no higher than for registered mortgages.

REPAYING THE MORTGAGE

Although most finance houses are happy to allow terms of up to 5 years for cheaper craft, or up to 10 years at the top end of the market, some may attach penalties to mortgage agreements to discourage early settlement. Since this policy varies from one finance house to another, it will be worthwhile including this point when comparing rates from one company to another.

7

INSURANCE

Although yacht insurance in this country is not compulsory, there is so much scope for damage to the yacht, the crew, or other vessels in the ordinary course of navigation that it would be foolish not to have comprehensive insurance cover.

Unlike the simple form of contract used in household and motor car insurance, the standard yacht insurance policy is a complex document. It is difficult for the layman to understand the contract fully without access to the Marine Insurance Act 1906 and the body of marine insurance case law contained in the Lloyds law reports.

The yacht insurance market is highly competitive, divided between a number of Lloyds underwriters (who may only be approached via Lloyds brokers) and insurance companies (who may be approached either through brokers or direct). In the insurance market as anywhere else you get what you pay for, and while it is wise to shop around you should not be tempted to go for the underwriter or company offering the lowest premium for that reason alone. Experience has shown that underwriters and companies away from the cheaper end of the market tend to be more flexible in interpreting the strict terms of the policy in the case of difficult claims, and speedier in settling the more straightforward ones.

With a wide variety of companies, brokers and underwriters competing in the market, and the great range of policies and policy wording on offer, it is sometimes difficult to make valid comparisons on a value-for-money basis.

When a broker is approached for a quotation, he will usually quote a figure between 1% and 2.5% of the declared value of the craft. There is always room for negotiation over premium rates, as the nature of risk varies according to a number of factors. Is the mooring secure against extremes of weather? Is the area patrolled by police or harbour officials to discourage vandalism and theft? What is the intended cruising range? Does the owner have any significant qualifications? Has the craft been built to current BW or NRA standards (and does the insurer regard that as relevant)? Is the owner prepared to carry a reasonable excess? (an agreement to pay the first £250 can make a big difference to the premium). Is the owner a member of a club that entitles him to a discount?

Most underwriters will be happy to insure a yacht up to 10 years old, without a survey being required.

It is essential when completing the proposal form to put in the fullest and most accurate information and to answer all the questions literally. The proposal form constitutes the basis of a binding contract, and in the event of a claim, most underwriters will re-examine the proposal to ensure that the claim is valid within its terms of reference. The law recognises that insurance contracts are one-sided; the boatowner knows everything about himself, his boat and the nature of his proposed use of the boat. Since the insurer only knows what the owner chooses to tell him, he is protected by the principle of *uberrima fides*. Roughly translated this means that the insured must show the "utmost good faith" in providing information, failure to do so will entitle the insurer to avoid the contract even if a subsequent claim is entirely irrelevant to the subject matter of the false statement.

So far as the average UK-based boatowner is concerned, there are three main cruising ranges available at standard prices which must be declared on a proposal form, these are:

(a) non-tidal waters within the UK;
(b) coastal cruising within an agreed range of the yacht's home port or permanent mooring;
(c) full coastal and sea-going cruising within the "home trade" limits, which cover all UK waters and continental coasts from Brest to Elbe, (some policies may include continental inland waters as far south as Paris, but an additional premium is usually payable).

Particularly in the case of fast motorboats (insurers normally attach special conditions to boats capable of 17 knots or more) security against theft, or against the weather while at a mooring or at anchor is a major concern to insurers. They will usually insist that if a trailed boat is not kept at home, it must be made secure in a locked compound, and if left afloat unattended, must at all times be on a secure and reasonably sheltered mooring.

Unlike motor insurance, where the value of a car in the event of a write-off is taken to be its current market value, marine insurance is based on the principle of agreed value. If a yacht is insured for, say, £10,000, and in the case of total loss the insurers are able to show that it would have fetched no more than £8000 on the open market, they are still liable to pay the full figure. Provided the insured has not deliberately over stated the value, there should be no argument on the matter. This does not of course exempt him from accurately stating the price paid on the proposal form; this is not necessarily the same as the value of the yacht, although insurers may wish to know the reason for any difference in these figures.

Underwriters will of course need to be informed of any intention to use the yacht for charter, whether bareboat or skippered, or for any commercial purpose. While this is not a problem in itself, underwriters will normally lay down conditions about the qualifications and experience of prospective charterers.

Under the speedboat clauses in most policies, any use for racing or speed trials is specifically excluded, and special insurance should be taken out with the club organising any such event.

Difficulties can arise when an owner forgets to lay up (or re-launch) his yacht on the date stated on the proposal form. Claims have been turned down by underwriters on the grounds that the nature of risks while afloat are very different to those ashore. While most insurers are flexible about varying lay-up and relaunch dates, it is wise to inform them in advance of any proposed variation.

So far as third party liability is concerned, most standard policies provide the owner with indemnity up to £500,000, or in some cases £1m. It should be remembered that these high figures will rarely be approached, even in the case of a bad accident, as the Merchant Shipping Act Limitation of Liability provisions will normally apply. The effect of the limitation provisions is to allow a yacht owner (or his insurers) to limit liability for third-party property damage to about £60,000, and for death or personal injury to about £120,000. However, since limitation does not apply to guests or passengers injured aboard the insured's own craft, it is as well to carry substantial insurance against such misfortune.

An increasing number of harbour boards and navigation authorities are imposing third-party insurance requirements, and this trend is likely to continue over the next few years. In this context an important aspect of the cover provided is the cost of raising and removing the wreck of an insured boat in the event of it sinking in the fairway of a harbour or in the main channel of a navigable river or canal.

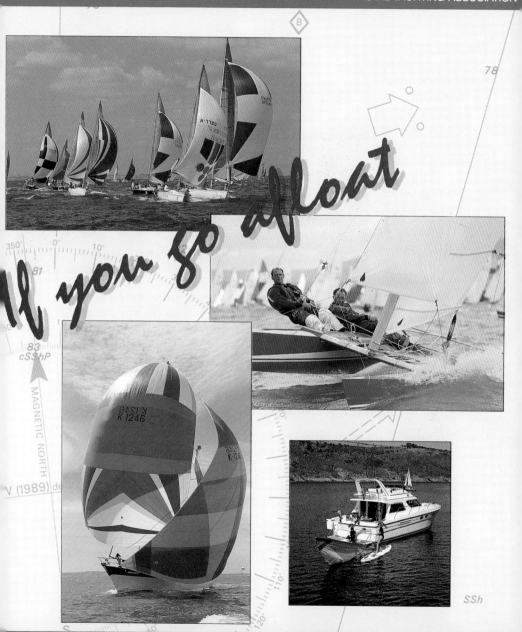

If you go afloat

The unique pleasures of being afloat are enjoyed by more people today than at any time in the past. The RYA is your national association, run and managed by people like you who enjoy the excitement of racing and the pleasures of cruising under power or sail.

We are here to help you, protect your interests, make your activities afloat safer and more enjoyable, and to provide really sound advice when you most need it. We manage training schemes which cater for everyone, from beginners to the most experienced, and improve the boating skills of many thousands of enthusiasts on courses every year. Our work on the rights of navigation, buoyage, and access to water, benefits you every time you go afloat. And when you take your boat abroad we can make the paperwork simple and provide the advice you need

The RYA is run by its members and funded by their subscriptions. Every additional member increases the influence we have in our work. Your membership is essential in enabling the RYA to negotiate effectively at national and international level as an organisation representing the 3 million people who participate in our sport.

By joining the RYA and flying our flag you will also be adding your valuable support to the freedom of boat owners to cruise – wherever they wish.

Joining today makes sense.

Membership Application Form

PLEASE USE BLOCK CAPITALS

Name
Mr/Mrs/Miss

Address

Postcode

Type of Membership Required (tick as applicable)

☐ **Personal** £16pa (or £15 if you pay by Direct Debit)

☐ **Junior** (under 21) £5pa Date of Birth

Signed

My principal boating interest is: (tick 1 box only)

Sail Cruising ☐   Sail Racing ☐   Windsurfing ☐   Motor Cruising ☐   Powerboat Racing ☐

THE EASY WAY TO PAY Direct Debit Instruction

Originators identification number: 955213

Please complete parts 1 to 5 to instruct your bank or building society to make payments directly from your account.
Then return the form to: Royal Yachting Association, RYA House, Romsey Road, Eastleigh, Hants SO5 4YA

DIRECT Debit

1. Name of account holder/s

2. Account number

3. Sort code

4. Please write the full postal address of your bank or building society branch in the box below.

To: The Manager   Bank

                                   Branch

Postcode

Banks or Building Societies may refuse to accept instructions to pay Direct Debits from some types of account.

5. **Your instructions to the bank or building society and signature**
- I instruct you to pay Direct Debits from my account at the request of the Royal Yachting Association.
- The amounts are variable and are to be debited on various dates.
- I understand that the Royal Yachting Association may change the amounts and dates only after giving me prior notice.
- I will inform the bank or building society in writing if I wish to cancel these instructions.
- I understand that if any Direct Debit is paid which breaks the terms of the instruction, the bank or building society will make a refund.

Signature(s):

Date:

OR CHEQUE/POSTAL ORDER/CASH *

enclosed for £   *please delete as applicable

Made payable to the Royal Yachting Association.

Office Use only:
Membership No. Allocated _____   7 7

Personal membership costs very little and you gain these direct benefits

Your Free Benefits

- **RYA NEWS**
  Our house magazine delivered to your home free of charge, quarterly.

- **SAIL NUMBERS**
  Allocation of a T, Y or M Series sail number.

- **HELMSMANS OVERSEAS CERTIFICATE OF COMPETENCE**
  Required by many EC countries and provided by the RYA to those of proven competence £15, or free to members.

- **LEGAL ADVICE ON ALL BOATING MATTERS**
  Our legal team is there to advise and support you on issues of boating law.

- **RYA LOUNGE AT THE LONDON INTERNATIONAL BOAT SHOW**
  Meet your friends – a place of refuge from the crowds with bar and restaurant.

- **THIRD PARTY INSURANCE FOR WINDSURFERS**
  Details on request.

- **FREE BOOK TOKEN**
  Worth a minimum of £5.00. select from a range of books shown in the RYA Catalogue.

- **RYA VISA CARD**
  A prestige card with no annual fee and very competitive terms.

Special Discounts

- **INSURANCE**
  10% or more with qualifications on most policies through RYA Brokers Bishop Skinner & Co Ltd.

- **HOSPITAL AND MEDICAL CARE ASSOCIATION**
  Up to 40% discount for RYA members.

- **CAR RENTAL**
  Specially negotiated discounts from Europcar Interrent.

See overleaf for membership

8

FINDING A MOORING

Much has been written in recent times about the shortage of mooring space in this country. This has been brought about by an increase of between 3 - 4,000 yachts built and imported each year, restrictive planning policies by local authorities controlling the development of new marinas, and the need of new yacht owners to find a mooring near large centres of population.

In fact there is ample space in our creeks, estuaries, rivers and harbours to provide moorings for two or three times the present numbers of small craft. The situation in certain defined areas is admittedly very tight; around the Solent space may be particularly expensive, but for those prepared to look a little further afield, to Poole, the Isle of Wight, along the Sussex coast or further West in Dorset there is much less pressure, with the further bonus of sailing in uncrowded waters. Elsewhere around the coast many of the more popular small harbours have reached capacity, or unfairly restrict the grant of mooring licences to local residents. There will however always be space, and normally at very much lower cost, in the less accessible and less obvious areas and harbours. Unless you are intent on joining a keen racing fleet, or are very short of time to spend on travelling to your mooring, you should consider a mooring away from the most congested and expensive areas.

Looking further afield, many boat owners have chosen marina berths on the Mediterranean coasts of France and Spain, and claim that in doing so they are saving money and have more time for sailing. With cheap flights available from Northern and Midland airports to areas with marina berthing available at one third to one quarter of the fees charged in the UK this can make a lot of sense, even taking into account the fact that VAT-free export to other EC States ceased to apply after 31st December 1992.

9

BUYING FOR USE ON INLAND WATERS

Although there have been construction and equipment regulations in force on the River Thames since the mid-1920's, regulations for privately-owned craft on waters controlled by British Waterways, the Norfolk and Suffolk Broads Authority and other NRA waters (the Medway and Anglian rivers) are a very new concept, and will need to be complied with if it is intended to base a boat on those waters.

The three navigation authorities, in cooperation with the British Marine Industries Federation, have developed a training course and qualification scheme for inspectors. The intention is that a navigation licence or registration certificate will only be issued for craft that have a current certificate of compliance issued by an authorised inspector. The Boat Standards that were finally agreed in 1993 after lengthy consultation between the authorities and the main user organisations are unlikely to become compulsory for BW waters until mid-1994, and on the Broads before 1995. Nevertheless if it is intended to base a boat in any of these areas, it makes sense to ensure that it complies with the detailed requirements of the new standards.

Copies of which are available on request from:

British Waterways Board
Willow Grange
WATFORD
WD1 3QA

National Rivers Authority
Kings Meadow House
Kings Meadow Road
READING
RG1 8DQ

Broads Authority
Thomas Harvey House
18 Colegate
Norwich
NORFOLK
NR3 1BQ

BUYING FOR COMMERCIAL USE

Reference has been made to new regulations being introduced by the Department of Transport for commercially-used pleasure craft. Most of the Merchant Shipping legislation laying down rules for the design, construction and equipment of ships specifically exempts pleasure yachts or pleasure craft from compliance. However the *Marques* incident in 1985, in which a converted trading schooner capsized and sank with serious loss of life in a Tall Ships Race, has led to the DoT amending the rules to exclude commercially used yachts from exemption, and to require them to comply with a stringent Code of Practice. The regulations will be fully in force from 1994 onwards.

Yachts used bona fide for the private pleasure of an owner or his family or friends, or within a club syndicate, will be exempt, provided that any contribution to costs is for running expenses only. Any charters, whether crewed or bare-boat, will bring a yacht within the new regulations, (unless the charter is primarily for racing purposes), and indeed any other commercial purpose will also necessitate compliance with the Code of Practice.

The regulations will cover various areas of operation, in 5 categories from less than 20 miles from a safe haven, to unrestricted service, and will encompass all aspects of design and equipment, including stability requirements, weathertightness, requirement for diesel engine, detailed electrical arrangements, fire prevention requirements, and lifesaving and safety equipment.

Many of these requirements will certainly be expensive to comply with, and undoubtedly go far beyond what has conventionally been considered adequate for cruising yachts in the past. Any prospective owner considering subsidising his costs by occasional chartering (let alone running the yacht on a full-time charter basis) should study the Code of Practice in detail with the builder, and draw up detailed costings of the additional construction and equipment requirements, before entering into a binding contract to buy the yacht.

Details of the Code of Practice for craft up to 24 metres can be obtained from: **Department of Transport Marine Directorate Spring Place 105 Commercial Road Southampton SO1 0ZD**

APPENDIX I

AGREEMENT FOR THE SALE
OF A SECONDHAND YACHT

An agreement prepared by the Royal Yachting Association for the sale of a secondhand yacht between persons not normally engaged in the business of selling yachts.

AN AGREEMENT made the………day of…………19…………..

BETWEEN :

1. "The Vendor" : ....

of ....

2. "The Purchaser" : ....

of ....

The terms "Vendor" and "Purchaser" include their respective successors in title and the Vendor and Purchaser shall hereinafter be collectively referred to as "the Parties".

"The Purchase Price" : £.......................sterling

"The Deposit" ....: 10% of the Purchase Price

In respect of the sale of a [REGISTERED/UNREGISTERED] PLEASURE CRAFT

Name : ....

Description : ....

Official No. : ....

Port of Registry where applicable : ....

Now lying at : ....
Including all equipment, machinery and gear on board ("the Yacht") and any specific inventory attached hereto initialled by the Parties and forming part of this Agreement.

1. **Agreement for sale**
   The Vendor hereby agrees to sell and the Purchaser agrees to purchase the Yacht free from any encumbrances (subject to the conditions and terms of this agreement), together with all her outfit gear and equipment as set out in a schedule hereto but not including stores or the Vendor's personal effects, for the Purchase Price.

2. **Payment of deposit**
   On the signing of this agreement the Deposit is to be paid to the Vendor and the balance of the Purchase Price together with any Value Added Tax shall be payable in accordance with Clause 6.

3.1 **Value Added Tax**
   The Vendor [is/is not] a registered person for the purpose of the regulations relating to Value Added Tax and the Purchase Price [is/is not] exclusive of Value Added Tax.

3.2 **Import dues and local taxes (craft lying overseas)**
   The Vendor warrants that the craft has been into [   ] and that all appropriate local taxes and dues have been paid and that the proposed sale is in accordance with all relevant local laws and regulations.

4. **Inspection survey**
   The Purchaser may, at a venue to be agreed and at his own cost, haul out or place ashore and/or open up the Yacht and her machinery for the purposes of inspection and/or survey which, including any written report, shall be completed within [   ] days of the signing of this agreement. If any inspection requires more than superficial non-destructive dismantling the consent of the Vendor must be obtained before such work commences.

5.1 **Notice of defects**
   Within fourteen days after completion of such inspection and/or survey if any material defect(s) in the Yacht or her machinery other than disclosed to the Purchaser in writing prior to the signing of this agreement or any material deficiencies in her inventory, if any, shall have been found the Purchaser may either :

5.1.1 give notice to the Vendor of his rejection of the Yacht provided that the notice shall specify any material defect(s) or deficiencies; or

5.1.2 give notice to the Vendor specifying any material defect(s) or deficiencies and requiring the Vendor forthwith either to make good the same or make a sufficient reduction in the Purchase Price to enable the Purchaser to make good the same. All agreed items of work to be completed without undue delay in all circumstances and to be carried out so as to satisfy the expressly specified requirements of the Purchaser's surveyor in respect only of material defects mentioned in his report and specified in the notice to the Vendor.

5.2 If the Purchaser shall have served a notice of rejection under Clause 5.1.1, then this agreement shall be deemed to be rescinded forthwith and the Vendor shall refund to the purchaser the Deposit in accordance with Clause 8.

5.3 If the Purchaser shall have served a notice under Clause 5.1.2 requiring the Vendor to make good material defects or deficiencies or to make a reduction in the Purchase Price, and the Vendor shall not have agreed within twenty one days after the service of the notice to make good such defects or the Parties have not agreed in the twenty one days after the service of notice upon the reduction in the Purchase Price, then this agreement shall be deemed to have been rescinded on the twenty second day after the service of notice and the Vendor shall refund to the Purchaser the Deposit in accordance with Clause 8.

In the case of any deficiencies in the Yacht's inventory (if any) remaining or arising within seven days of acceptance in accordance with Clause 6 the deficiencies shall be made good or a reduction in the Purchase Price shall be agreed, failing which this agreement shall be rescinded at the option of the Purchaser only.

6.1 Acceptance of yacht
The Yacht shall be deemed to have been accepted by the Purchaser and the balance of the Purchase Price and any Value Added Tax thereon shall become due and payable in

accordance with Clause 7 upon the happening of any of the following events :

6.2 The expiry of fourteen days from the date of this agreement or such extended period as may be agreed between the Parties provided that no inspection or survey has been commenced;

6.3 The expiry of fifteen days from the completion of the survey, provided that the Purchaser has not served notice under Clause 5.1;

6.4 Notification in writing by the Vendor to the Purchaser of completion of the remedial works specified in a notice given by the Purchaser under Clause 5.1.2;

7.1 Completion of sale
Upon acceptance of the Yacht by the Purchaser, the Deposit shall be treated as part payment of the Purchase Price. Within seven days of acceptance the Purchaser shall pay the balance of the Purchase Price and any Value Added Tax thereon and the Vendor shall :

In the case of a registered yacht

7.1.1 Registered yacht
provide the Purchaser with the Certificate of Registry, correct and updated, together with any other documents appertaining to the Yacht and shall execute a Bill of Sale, in the prescribed form, in favour of the Purchaser or his nominee, showing the Yacht to be free from encumbrances and completed so as to ensure transfer on the Register;

OR

7.1.2 In the case of an unregistered yacht
(including a yacht registered on the SSR)

(a)   Provide the Purchaser with a Bill of Sale in favour of the Purchaser or his nominee, together with any other   documents appertaining to the Yacht;

(b)   Deliver to the Purchaser any necessary delivery

order or other authority enabling the Purchaser to take immediate possession of the Yacht.

7.2 Where payment is made by cheque, draft, letter of credit or other instrument, the terms of this agreement shall not be deemed to have been fulfilled until such payment is cleared into the payee's account.

7.3 Vendor's right to assign title
By delivery of the documents specified in either case the Vendor shall be deemed to have covenanted AND HEREBY COVENANTS that he has the right to transfer property in the Yacht and that the same is free from all encumbrances, debts, liens and the like except such encumbrances and liabilities for duties, taxes, debts, liens and the like as are the responsibility of the Purchaser under Clauses 4 and 8.

7.4 Free access after completion
On completion, the Vendor shall ensure that the Yacht is available for collection by the Purchaser and that free access by the Purchaser together with all necessary haulage equipment is permitted at no additional cost to the Purchaser.

8.1 Rescission of agreement
In the event of rescission of this agreement by the Purchaser he shall, at his own expense, reinstate the Yacht to the condition and position in which he found her, and shall pay all boatyard and surveyor's charges for this work.

8.2 Return of deposit
The Vendor shall thereupon return the Deposit to the Purchaser without deduction and without interest save that he shall be entitled to retain such part of the Deposit as shall be necessary to defray any boatyard or surveyor's charges not paid by the Purchaser.

Neither party shall thereafter have any claim against the other under this agreement.

9.   Warranties
The Vendor being a person not selling the Yacht in the course of a business, and the Purchaser being at liberty to inspect the Yacht and satisfy himself as to her condition and

specification, all express or implied warranties or conditions, statutory or otherwise, are hereby excluded and the Yacht, her outfit, gear and equipment shall be taken with all defects and faults of description without any allowance or abatement whatsoever.

10.   Risk

Until the Yacht has been accepted or shall be deemed to have been accepted by the Purchaser she shall be at the risk of the Vendor who shall make good all damage sustained by her before the date of acceptance. If the Yacht be lost or becomes a constructive total loss before such acceptance, this agreement shall be null and void except that the Purchaser will be liable for the cost of all work authorised by him under Clauses 4 and 8 and undertaken before such loss took place and the Deposit shall be returned to the Purchaser without interest but less any deduction made under Clauses 4 and 8 and otherwise without deduction and the Purchaser shall have no claim against the Vendor for damages or otherwise. After acceptance the Yacht shall in all respects be at the risk of the Purchaser.

Notwithstanding the provisions of this clause the ownership of the Yacht will not vest in the Purchaser until payment of the balance of the Purchase Price in accordance with Clause 7 even though the Purchaser may have insured his risk under the provisions of this clause.

11.1 Default by purchaser

Should the Purchaser fail to pay the balance of the Purchase Price in accordance with Clause 7, the Vendor may give notice in writing to the Purchaser requiring him to complete the purchase within fourteen days of the service of such notice.

If the Purchaser fails to comply with the notice then the Vendor may re-sell the Yacht by public auction or private treaty and any deposit paid shall thereupon be forfeit without prejudice to the Vendor's right to claim from the Purchaser the amount of any loss on re-sale together with all his reasonable costs and expenses, due allowance being made for any forfeited deposit. On the expiry of the said notice the Yacht shall be at the Vendor's risk.

11.2 Default by vendor

If the Vendor shall default in the execution of his part of the contract the Purchaser shall, without prejudice to any other rights he may have hereunder, be entitled to the return of the Deposit.

Unless such default by the Vendor shall have arisen from events over which the Vendor had no control, the Vendor shall pay interest upon the amount of the Deposit for the period during which he has held it at the rate of 4% per annum above finance house base rate, together with compensation for any loss which the Purchaser may have sustained as a result of the Vendor's default.

12. Arbitration

All disputes that cannot be resolved between the Parties and which arise out of or in connection with this agreement shall be submitted to a single arbitrator to be appointed, in default of agreement, by the Chairman of the Council of the RYA and the provisions of the Arbitration Act 1950 (as amended) shall apply.

13. Notices

Any notice under this agreement shall be in writing and any notice to the Purchaser or Vendor shall be sufficiently served if delivered to him personally or posted by recorded delivery to his last known address. Any notice posted shall be deemed to have been received forty eight hours after the time of posting and any notice given in any other manner shall be deemed to have been received at the time when, in the ordinary course of post, it may be expected to have been received.

14. Jurisdiction

This agreement shall be construed according to, and governed by the Law of England (or of Scotland if the Vendor's address shall be in that country) and the Parties hereby submit to the jurisdiction of the Courts of the same countries.

15. Marginal notes

The construction of this agreement is not to be affected by any marginal notes.

16. Rights under contract or statute

This agreement forms the entire agreement between the Parties unless otherwise specifically agreed in writing between them.

SIGNED BY THE VENDOR ....

In the presence of : ....

SIGNED BY THE PURCHASER...

In the presence of : ....

APPENDIX 2

AGREEMENT FOR THE SYNDICATE OWNERSHIP OF A YACHT

AN AGREEMENT made the...............day of ....19............

BETWEEN..........................of......................................

("the first owner")

and.................................of.......................................

("the second owner")

The owners include their respective successors in title and shall hereinafter be collectively referred to as "the Parties".

WHEREAS the Parties wish to enter into an agreement to share the management and use of the yacht .... (the Yacht)

[and **WHEREAS** the first owner is the present owner of the Yacht]

[and **WHEREAS** the second owner has by a prior contract purchased from the first owner /64ths of the Yacht]

[and **WHEREAS** the Parties have jointly and severally purchased the Yacht in the following shares :

the first owner purchasing   /64ths

the second owner purchasing   /64ths

and **WHEREAS** the parties have jointly and severally entered into an agreement with [   ] (the "Mortgage Company")].

NOW IT IS HEREBY MUTUALLY AGREED between the Parties as follows :

1. **Joint bank account**
   The first owner shall forthwith open a [Bank/ Building Society] account ("the Account") in the names of the Parties into which the Parties shall upon the [　] day of [　] in each year transfer the amount of £[　　] until six months after the termination of this agreement in accordance with Clause 5.

2. **Withdrawals and contributions from/to account**
   The first [and second] owner/s shall have power [jointly/ separately] to draw monies from the Account for the sole purpose of the maintenance and management of the Yacht as [he/they] shall in their absolute discretion think fit and shall have power to call for further and necessary contributions in equal shares from [the second owner/each other] subject always to the safeguards in Clause 4.7 and to the general law affecting principal and agent.

3. **Casual disbursements**
   Any disbursement, payment or account discharged by one owner on behalf of the other and of the general management of the yacht shall from time to time as convenient but certainly once annually be reported to the other owner and each owner jointly and severally agrees to contribute one half of such disbursements, payments or accounts upon proper documentation in the form of receipts, etc. being presented as evidence of payment.

4. **Management responsibility**
   The first owner shall have the following powers, duties and responsibilities :

4.1 to make day-to-day decisions for the general management of the Yacht;

4.2 to make (after consultation with the second owner) any arrangement for the purchase of capital equipment such as sails, engines etc. as may be necessary and for any agreement to charter the Yacht;

4.3 to insure the Yacht, her apparel, fittings etc. against the usual risks either at Lloyds or with an insurance company or association;

4.4 to employ any yard, sail-loft, brokers or agents on their usual terms of business and to transact any necessary business in relation to the Yacht;

4.5 to make, adjust, apportion or settle at his discretion any salvage, damage, average or other claims in favour of or against the Yacht or to refer the same to arbitration;

4.6 to take such steps as may be necessary to defend proceedings, accept service or arrange finance relating to the Yacht;

4.7 as soon as reasonably practicable after the [ ] day of [ ] in each year to render to the second owner accounts paid together with the Account statements as evidence of payment, and on request to produce all vouchers, books or other documents and papers relating to the management of the Account and of the Yacht.

5. **Termination of agreement**
If either of the Parties has reasonable cause or desire to terminate this agreement, he may, by individual notice in writing to the other party, indicate his desire to terminate. Such termination shall take place within six months after the delivery of such notice in writing.

Upon such notice in writing being delivered, the other party shall take such steps as may be necessary to secure the execution of a proper release and indemnity against all liabilities contracted by the determining party and shall arrange to purchase the share of the determining party at a fair market price or alternatively obtain agreement by another to take on the share of the determining party. Likewise, the determining party hereby agrees to defray or settle all his share of the disbursements, payments or accounts for the Yacht up to and including the date of actual termination as agreed between the Parties which for the avoidance of doubt may be any date within six months of the individual notice in writing being received by the other party.

If a dispute arises as to the price to be paid to the determining party for his share then a valuation shall be obtained from a recognised yacht broker and in default of agreement then the entirety of the Yacht shall be publicly advertised for sale with notice of time and place for sale being given to both Parties and she shall be sold. Each of the Parties on receiving his share of the purchase money shall execute the necessary Bill of Sale of his share in the Yacht to the purchaser and deliver up possession of the Yacht. The costs of such sale shall be paid by the Parties according to their respective shares.

6. Where it is agreed to terminate this agreement and the Parties have mutually agreed to sell the Yacht, it shall then be sold either by private treaty at such price as the Parties may agree or, in default of such agreement, by public auction subject to such conditions as are usual on the sale of such yachts. Each of the Parties shall be at liberty to bid for and purchase the Yacht at any such public auction, or to purchase the Yacht outright for the price advertised for sale by private treaty.

7.1 Regular payment of mortgage etc.
In the case of a mortgage or hire purchase agreement being in operation each owner jointly and severally agrees to pay his monthly or other contribution to defray the costs of such mortgage or hire purchase agreement into the Account in accordance with Clause 1 until the date of determination agreed in accordance with Clause 5.

7.2 Final settlement of mortgage debt
In the event of the sale of the Yacht, each owner jointly and severally agrees with the other to defray from his share of the sale price his share of the mortgage or hire purchase agreement entered into with the Mortgage Company.

8. Arbitration
If any dispute, difference or question arises between the Parties relating to the rights, duties or obligations of either of them, including (without prejudice to the generality hereof) any dispute, difference or question whether the owners have, in fact, properly and satisfactorily carried out their obligations under this agreement, the same shall be referred to arbitration by a single arbitrator to be agreed upon by the Parties or, failing such agreement, appointed by the

Secretary-General of the RYA. This shall be deemed to be a submission to arbitration within the Arbitration Act 1950.

9. Any notice under this agreement shall be in writing and shall be sufficiently served if delivered personally or posted to the last known postal address in Great Britain or Ireland of either of the Parties.

IN WITNESS whereof this agreement has been signed by the Parties the day and year first above written

SIGNED BY THE FIRST OWNER ....

in the presence of : ....

SIGNED BY THE SECOND OWNER ....

in the presence of : ....

APPENDIX 3

BRITISH BOATING INDUSTRY CODE OF PRACTICE FOR THE SALE OF USED BOATS

SECTION FOUR

BROKER AND VENDOR/PURCHASER

1. **Legal liability to disclose information**
    (i) Vendors

    Brokers must incorporate into "instructions to sell" forms and/or particulars/questionnaire forms, a clause to the effect:

    "The Vendor declares that to the best of his knowledge and belief the particulars given to the broker and signed or supplied by the Vendor are correct, and that he has power to dispose of the vessel with the concurrence of any joint owner or mortgagee or hire purchase company and all known defects have been declared and that he understands the implications of the Misrepresentations Act of 1976 and agrees to indemnify the Broker against all costs, claims and demands arising in consequence of any of the information given in the particulars being incorrect."

    (ii) Brokers

    The Broker is responsible for providing accurate information to the best of his ability, and defects or deficiencies in a boat of which the Broker is aware must be divulged to Purchasers and the Vendor. (See paragraph 2 (iii) of Section 3)

2. **Central Agencies (Sole Agents)**
    Central Agency instructions from Vendors must be in writing and must be produced by the Central Agent on request of another Member. If a Vendor states his intention of appointing only one agent, but reserves the right to sell his boat privately, this is not a Central Agency.

3. **Offers**
In the absence of express agreement to the contrary, the Vendor's approval to sell must be obtained even when the asking price has been offered and all offers must be submitted until such time as a deposit acceptable to the Vendor is paid and the terms agreed by the Vendor.

4. **Contract**
An Agreement for the Sale and Purchase of a Second Hand Yacht on a recognised ABYA approved form should always be used, but, in the absence of such an agreement, it is recommended that Brokers establish a contract in the form of a receipt or otherwise by memorandum. Such receipt or memorandum should state that any deposit paid is deemed to be held on the terms of the said ABYA approved form.

5. **Quoted prices**
Brokers must not offer boats at a lower figure than that quoted by the Vendor. The price quoted shall be in all cases the gross price inclusive of commission. Where applicable, any VAT liability must be indicated in accordance with current legislation.

6. **Surveys**
Other than in exceptional circumstances, a Broker should always advise a Purchaser to have a survey. However, a Broker should not recommend a particular surveyor but may accept the Purchaser's instructions to appoint a surveyor on his behalf. On no account shall the Broker make or receive a commission in connection with the survey.

7. **Sale proceeds**
The Broker shall be responsible for keeping the deposit, part payments and the proceeds of the sale in a separate banking account designated for the purpose, and shall account for the same to the Vendor after deducting such commission as may be properly due to the Broker or his Sharing Broker within fourteen days of the sale being effected, or where applicable after transfer of clear title to the Purchaser, whichever shall be later.

8. **Title and registration**
At the time of the sale the Lead Broker shall obtain evidence

of title a properly executed Bill of Sale or receipt showing the boat to be free from encumbrances, which shall be exchanged for the cleared purchase monies for the boat. Brokers are required to provide the facility, at a reasonable extra charge, to their clients for dealing with British Registration procedures and Customs Documentation.

*(Practice Note: While a Purchaser or Vendor is not obliged to engage a Broker to transfer ownership of a registered vessel, the Broker is strongly advised to encourage the Purchaser and Vendor to appoint him for this purpose, and it is recommended that only modest fees be charged for this service on order to encourage continuity of Registration.)

9.   Standard disclaimer for particulars

It is recommended that the following wording is included in any particulars shown to a prospective purchaser.

"In this case we are acting as Brokers only. The Vendor is/ is not selling in the course of business. [Delete as necessary.] Whilst every care has been taken in their preparation, the correctness of these particulars is not guaranteed. The particulars are intended only as a guide and they do not constitute a term of any contract. A prospective buyer is strongly advised to check the particulars and where appropriate, at his own expense to employ a qualified marine surveyor to carry out a survey and/or to have an engine trial conducted."

*(Practice Note: This disclaimer will not be appropriate in all circumstances and care should be taken to ensure that it is suitably amended and/or deleted as necessary, for example; in the case where the Broker is acting as a principal; where the Vendor is selling in the course of business; where VAT is payable; if an engine is not fitted and so on.)

APPENDIX 4

LEADING MARINE FINANCE HOUSES GIVING UNREGISTERED MORTGAGES.

British Credit Trust Ltd
34 High Street
Slough
Berkshire
SL1 1ED

Forward Trust Ltd
12 Calthorpe Road
Edgbaston
Birmingham
B15 1QZ

Lombard North Central (Marine) Plc
371 Millbrook Road
Southampton
Hampshire
SO1 0HW

NWS Bank Plc
Alleyn House
23/27 Carlton Crescent
Southampton
Hampshire
SO1 2EU

Royscot Finance
Edward House
289 West Campbell Street
Glasgow
G2 4UG

APPENDIX 5

BILL OF SALE

for the Yacht	....' ('the Yacht')
Type:	....
Year built:	....
Length:	....
Beam:	....
Auxiliary Power:	....
Small Ships Reg. No:	....

                    ....   [and   ....

of: ....   of: ....

         ....]

                                    ('the Transferor[s]')

IN CONSIDERATION of the sum of £......................
(............................. pounds) paid to me/us by:

                    ....   [and   ....

of: ....   of: ....

         ....]

                                   ('the Transferee[s]')

receipt of which is acknowledged;

1. **Transfer** the Yacht to the Transferee[s];
2. For myself/ourselves and for my/our heirs **covenant** with the Transferee[s] and his/ their heirs and assigns that I/we have power so to transfer and that the Yacht is free from encumbrances.

SIGNED this..................day of ....19[   ]

                .... (signature of Transferor[s])

         [........................]

in the presence of:

                .... (signature of Witness)

                .... (name of Witness)

of: .... (address of Witness)

Notes:
1. This form of Bill of Sale may be used on the transfer of an un-registered yacht or a yacht registered on the Small Ships Register. Transfers of yachts registered under Part 1 of the 1894 Merchant Shipping Act should be evidenced using the Bill of Sale prescribed by HM Customs & Excise.
2. Please delete inapplicable alternatives.
3. This form of Bill of Sale should not be used when transfer is by gift, or if any of the parties to it is a corporate body.
4. Separate copies of this draft Bill of Sale (in A4 format) are available to **personal members of the RYA** on request.

APPENDIX 6

USEFUL ADDRESSES AND TELEPHONE NUMBERS

British Marine Industries Federation
Meadlake Place, Thorpe Lea Road, Egham
Surrey TW20 8HE
Tel: 0784 473377

Registrar General of Shipping and Seamen
Government Buildings, St Agnes Road, Gabalfa
Cardiff CF4 4YA
Tel: 0222 586203

Registrar of British Ships (London)
HM Customs and Excise, Dorset House, Stamford Street
London SE1 9PS
Tel: 071 202 4078/4079/4080

Registrar of British Ships (Southampton)
HM Customs and Excise, Custom House, Orchard Place
Southampton SO9 1ZD
Tel: 0703 827082

DVLA Small Ships Register
Swansea, SA99 1BX
Tel: 0792 783355

Royal Yachting Association
RYA House, Romsey Road, Eastleigh, Hampshire SO5 4YA
Tel: 0703 629962

Yacht Brokers, Designers and Surveyors Association
Wheel House, Petersfield Road, Whitehill, Borden
Hampshire GU35 9BU
Tel: 0420 473862

HM Customs and Excise
Dorset House, Stamford Street
London SE1 9PS
Tel: 071 202 4078/4079/4080

APPENDIX 7

TAXATION RATES IN EC STATES
(AS AT FEBRUARY 1993)

BELGIUM

VAT 19.5% on new or imported boats. "First Registration" tax of 2500 ECU payable on new boats above 7.5m. Registration tax of 25% on used boats at each re-sale.

DENMARK

VAT payable on full value of boat when dealer is involved in transaction in force. VAT rate 25%. Light and navaid tax based on 1% of insurance value in force.

FRANCE

VAT at 18%. Tax on all users of inland waterways under consideration. Annual user tax based on engine power greater than 5 h.p. and hull size (greater than 3GRT) in force.

GERMANY

Tax on dealer's margin in force. VAT on new boats 15% in force.

GREECE

VAT on new boats 18%, and 3.6% on used boats in force.

IRELAND

VAT at 21%.

ITALY

VAT at 19% up to 50 tonnes and 38% over 50 tonnes in force.

NETHERLANDS 17.5% VAT in force.

PORTUGAL

VAT at 16% for all types of boats. annual user tax depending on length and engine power.

SPAIN

VAT at 15% on all boats plus a 13% registration tax on boats over 7.5m. This is compulsory for Spanish nationals and to all others who wish to register their boat in Spain.

UK

VAT at 17.5% on all UK goods and services.